I COULD HAVE GOTTEN THAT VIA EMAIL

Charisse Lewis, MBA

About the Author

Charisse Lewis, MBA

Systems and Leadership Consultant /Career Coach

Charisse Lewis is an accomplished Improvement Advisor/Systems and Leadership Consultant, Facilitator and Team Building/Team Development trainer who spent 13 years improving efficiency and workflows in the healthcare using LEAN six sigma tools and building relationships developing industry hundreds of teams over the years, and 10 years in the workforce development industry working with the "Hard to Serve" workforce population, teaching career guidance.

Working her way up the corporate ladder with no degree, in 2008 she became a certified Improvement Advisor, earning her six-sigma black belt and eventually graduating from the University of Canterbury with an MBA in Applied Management in 2011, a long way from humble beginnings of a 19-year-old mother. Charisse loves to role model that "can do" spirit and don't give up on what you want in life.

Some readers might think about these habits basic. I encourage you to ask yourself if you're truly applying these concepts to every and each meeting you attend. If not, you've got space to improve. Implementing these habits may be a good way to improve your effectiveness fast. If you maintain all of those habits, you may learn that meetings are an efficient tool to get work done.

Contents

About the Author ....

1. Get Written Agenda Ahead 1

2. Review the Attendee List 3

3. Manage the Meeting by the Clock 5

4. Use The "Parking Lot" To Manage Off Topic Discussions 7

5. Prewire Important Points and Decisions 9

6. Take Notes for Yourself 10

7. Follow Up on the Meeting 12

Running Effective Meetings 13

Plan out a Meeting Agenda 16

Prepare People to Actively Listen 19

Make Meetings More Comprehensive 22

Leave Meetings with Clear Next Steps and Owners 25

Charisse Lewis

 **1**

Get Written Agenda Ahead

Vague intentions to have a discussion on a topic seldom end on a productive note. If you're simply getting started with agendas, begin with a point form list of topics to be discussed and make certain that material is provided to attendees at least one day before the meeting. For higher results, provide background info on the agenda topics in order to have everyone attending well-informed.

What if you are asked to attend a meeting without an agenda? Simply ask, "Can you please provide an agenda for the upcoming meeting so that I can be prepare?"

Golden Tip: For frequently held meetings like a weekly status meeting on a project, you'll be able to save time by making a meeting template. Once you've got that

@mjcsolutions

I Could Have Gotten That Via Email

in place, preparing an agenda becomes a matter of filling in the blanks.

Charisse Lewis

Review the Attendee List

The individuals in the meeting space build or break your effectiveness. I even have been in hundreds meetings where the key person – a manager or executive – isn't present. As a result, no vital decisions can be made. Which was a waste of everyone's time.

For Meeting Organizers: limit the amount of individuals attending the meeting. The goal of meetings is to make decisions, provide and obtain results. For the most part, meetings aren't the best way to merely share info (exception: meetings are useful to share sensitive information)

For Meeting Attendees: browse the attendant list before you walk into the room. Be sure all the right people to make decisions are present: think about looking them up in your organization's directory (or on LinkedIn). Surprises aren't your friend once the meeting

@mjcsolutions

I Could Have Gotten That Via Email

gets going. Unexpected guests can sometimes derail your meeting.

Charisse Lewis

 **3**

Manage the Meeting by the Clock

Watching the clock is vital in an effective meeting. Once no one takes charge of managing time, it's simple to become careless and unfocused. Bear in mind – once individuals attend a meeting that's not well prepared, they check out and don't participate and are usually on Instagram. Make the time count!

For Meeting Organizers: Begin the meeting on time and ending on time (or a couple of minutes early!) This process can quickly enhance your reputation as an organized professional. If you're running an oversized or complex meeting, think about asking a colleague to serve as time keeper. If managing meetings to the clock is difficult for you, the parking lot habit (see #4 below) are going to be a game changer!

@mjcsolutions

I Could Have Gotten That Via Email

For Meeting Attendees:

Begin by arriving early at the meeting (I recommend five minutes for in-person conferences and 1-2 minutes for conference calls). Which means avoiding back to back commitments on your calendar whenever possible.

 **4**

Use The "Parking Lot" To Manage Off Topic Discussions

The first time I saw a meeting facilitator use a parking lot, I was so impressed. The parking lot performs 2 essential functions. First, it serves to keep the meeting targeted on the designated agenda. Second, the parking lot acknowledges ideas and issues raised by attendees, which is important so that people feel like they are being heard.

Golden Tip: The parking lot habit should be combined with the Follow Up habit if you would like to be actually effective. Otherwise, you're seemingly to achieve a reputation for merely making a show of acknowledging others.

As a meeting organizer, here are a couple of steps to use the parking lot concept.

I Could Have Gotten That Via Email

At the start of the meeting, explain your expectations to everybody to focus their discussions on the agenda. Further, explain that this rule can help the meeting stay productive and end on time.

Keep the meeting agenda document before of you as a guide.

Go through every agenda item

Monitor and contribute to the discussion

When somebody raises a stimulating point that doesn't relate to the agenda, say the following: "Thank you for that point, Tim. However, Microsoft Visual Studio tools go beyond the aim of this meeting. Let me write down that item in the "parking lot" and I can include it in the meeting notes that will be sent out by email so we will explore that point at the right time."

@mjcsolutions

 **5**

Prewire Important Points and Decisions

From time to time, major decisions are going to be discussed in meetings. It may be a decision on which projects to fund or which projects to cancel. Serious decisions like this need the pre-wiring habit. In essence, you communicate with individual one-on-one before the meeting regarding the decision before the meeting happens. Whereas time consuming, this approach will increase your probabilities of success (and avoids surprises other meeting attendees).

I Could Have Gotten That Via Email

Take Notes for Yourself

Taking notes in meetings is a necessary skill nonetheless I'm typically surprised by how often individuals forget to try and do it. The key reason to take notes in a meeting is to record any queries, action items or assignments that are directed to you. Let's inspect how attendees and organizers will act on notes.

Take notes in a paper notebook (e.g. a notebook or something similar) instead of using a pc, tablet or electronic device. Even though you've got fantastic skills to concentrate on the meeting, others might assume or get distracted that you just are "catching up on email" rather than capturing vital information and action items.

Taking notes for Meeting Organizers: If you propose to send minutes or an outline of the meeting to attendees, say this at the beginning of the meeting and explain what

Charisse Lewis

you may include. Sending out meeting minutes, even a couple of paragraphs or bullet points, may be a best practice.

Taking notes for Meeting Attendees: Bring a copy of the agenda and use that document to guide your note taking. Concentrate on the decisions made in the meeting and things that need any investigation or action on your part.

I Could Have Gotten That Via Email

7
Follow Up on the Meeting

The art and science of follow up is significant professional habit and it additionally matters within the context of meetings. Once it involves meeting tips, following up in a very timely basis may be a good way to manage stress and build a decent impression on others. For the simplest results, I recommend following up (e.g. making a telephone call, writing an email etc.) the same day as the meeting. For important matters, create a note on your calendar or task management tool of option to continue following up until you reach a resolution.

@mjcsolutions

Charisse Lewis

Running Effective Meetings

Understanding the way to have effective meetings is likely one in all the foremost vital skills professionals at all levels ought to learn to thrive at work. And yet, in line with on-line meeting provider Fuze, ineffective meetings waste an estimated $37 billion a year. A recent study in the Journal of Organizational Behavior found that, while delay is typically unacceptable in all other aspects of business life, "in the case of meetings, wasted time looks to be an accepted norm."

Meetings have attained a terrible reputation as a time suck, and it's no surprise. The general public tend to default to using meetings for one purpose: to share information while that can be essential generally, in reality, effective meeting strategies will help a team move work forward in a very important way—whether by gathering attendees to come

I Could Have Gotten That Via Email

back to a call, brainstorm new concepts, or workshop an answer to a problem.

Learning the way to run effective meetings isn't solely a benefit for productivity, however smart meetings also inspire bigger team collaboration which might have a direct result on the general happiness for team members and employees.

Here are 5 tips for running effective meetings, which can hopefully make them a lot more enjoyable.

Ask yourself: Is this meeting truly a meeting? Or can this be sent in an email?

Before even booking a space, ask yourself (or your team) if this meeting would be helpful to them and, if so, certain attendees actually must be present.

There are a couple of culprits disguising themselves as meeting-worthy, however the reality is that these meetings will typically be cropped down or skipped altogether.

Presentations: If the meeting is generally one person talking and a full bunch of individuals listening while attempting to not check their phones, it's seemingly more of a presentation than a meeting. To keep folks engaged, attempt passing out the slides before, then devote the majority of time to hosting a group discussion in person or on-line.

Status updates: Typically, these kinds of meetings are fast and to the point anyway, therefore why force individuals to interrupt their day? Save team members from context change by posting updates in a group message or maybe writing them on a whiteboard that the total team will see. Follow-up discussions will then happen with simply the individuals concerned in this specific project or activity.

I Could Have Gotten That Via Email

Plan out a Meeting Agenda

The first rule of running an effective meeting (once you've established whether your meeting is really a meeting) is to set an agenda. This lets individuals understand what to expect and might help table side discussions.

And if you are able to have a chosen facilitator to keep things buzzing on, that's AWESOME. "Experienced facilitators are key to flourishing meetings," says Jaffer. "They keep individuals on course, aren't afraid to interrupt, call out participants for being off-topic, and summarize the to-dos and next steps."

Some other Golden Tips for running effective meetings include:

Start meetings on time. Some meetings are scheduled for half-hour however are usually

Charisse Lewis

21 to 26 minutes long because individuals are checking email while looking forward to somebody to get there. At companies with over 250 individuals, nearly four-hundredth of meetings begin late. Even worse, the annoyance that grows while looking forward to the meeting begin spill over into the meeting itself, leading to a lot of interruptions, fewer concepts, and minimized morale. Crush that ill nature by getting started on time, even though everybody hasn't arrived.

Plan to engage individuals or check in on attendees every ten minutes. That's the typical span length, John Medina, a molecular biologist and author of Brain Rules, has found. As he puts it on his blog, "You've got 10 minutes with an audience before you may completely bore them. And you've got thirty seconds before they begin asking the question, 'Am I about to concentrate to you or not?' the moment you open your mouth, you're on the verge of getting your audience check out."

Assign individuals roles before the meeting starts. Having a facilitator and a dedicated note taker may be a smart place to begin. Or if you propose to engage specific individuals to talk on specific topics, make sure they're

@mjcsolutions

I Could Have Gotten That Via Email

briefed beforehand so that they will come into the meeting well versed in their material and prepared to share it.

How to have an efficient meeting:	Type of meeting and suggested meeting lengths
Meeting type:	Ideal meeting length
Regular team meeting:	15 to half-hour
Decision-making meeting:	A few hours, probably a full day depending on the decision
Brainstorming meeting:	40 minutes to one hour
Retrospective meeting:	30 minutes for each week in the project
One-on-one meeting:	30 minutes to one hour
Strategy meeting:	60 to 90 minutes

Charisse Lewis

Prepare People to Actively Listen

You've set to meet, made your invite list, and created an agenda. Great! On the day of the meeting, try and make the foremost of it by preparing individuals to essentially listen. "Active listening" is a communication technique—frequently utilized by counselors, teachers, and researchers—in that you listen deeply, and solely, to the speaker. Active listeners have an advantage instantly, absorbing the speakers words, gestures, and facial expressions, instead of merely looking forward to their turn to talk.

But to get individuals ready to pay attention actively, you'll have to set the scene a little bit. you'll be able to try this in some variety ways:

I Could Have Gotten That Via Email

Make the meeting setting comfortable. which may mean providing some food and drinks—if the meeting takes place first thing in the morning or over lunch—and ensuring the room is at a pleasurable temperature. Chairs ought to be quiet, and, when possible, book an area that has some natural light so that individuals don't get too comfortable.

Think about the optimum meeting time for your team. It's a decent plan to have some meetings for the morning when individuals have the foremost energy, or, as one study found, 2:30pm on a Tuesday work wonders.

It's no surprise that effective meetings need the eyes and ears of all meeting participants. So, before you dive into the agenda items, get attendees relaxed and receptive with a short icebreaker, whether it's some light physical activity to alleviate tension or a quick check-in on everyone's day or week.

Close those laptops and place phones out of arm's reach to scale back technological distractions. Don't trust individuals to prevent themselves from checking their phones: Science shows we literally can't help ourselves.

@mjcsolutions

Charisse Lewis

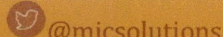@mjcsolutions

I Could Have Gotten That Via Email

Make Meetings More Comprehensive

Being comprehensive doesn't mean putting everybody in the company on the invite. Instead, think about inclusivity as a mindset. After you produce a secure area for individuals to express opinions—a place where people's concepts matter over their titles—work can (seemingly magically) get finished. By removing the power structure from the space, as Pixar co-founder Ed Catmull did in his meetings, you take away a stumbling block on the trail to creativity.

Just because everybody feels welcome at the meeting doesn't mean everybody needs to speak, though. There are some ways to keep individuals engaged.

Again, encourage team members to take written notes. Analysis shows that writing notes by hand helps

Charisse Lewis

individuals learn a lot, recall facts later, and gain a deeper understanding of the material than when they type notes.

Have people write down their questions throughout the meeting. Collect them and re-evaluate them as a group. This may facilitate introverts, or people who don't feel confident speaking up, get their issues addressed.

Break individuals into teams and have them accomplish little tasks, or make decisions, together. Then have them share their findings with the larger group.

Break the meeting into sections with a unique person leading every section or a part of the agenda. Switching up presenters helps refresh people's attention span and encourages attendees to feel accountable over a subject or project.

For groups with individuals operating remotely, you'll be able to beam them in via video conferencing for valuable face time. Make sure to meet at a time that's friendly to their time zone when possible which they'll see and listen to everybody clearly before you start. It's additionally a decent plan to provide dedicated space during the meeting when remote team members will participate, like during an

@mjcsolutions

I Could Have Gotten That Via Email

icebreaker question or different cluster activity. (You can set up virtual meeting rooms.

Charisse Lewis

Leave Meetings with Clear Next Steps and Owners

Some meetings leave us drained, whereas others might leave us impressed and wanting more. If you've planned well, who knows—your meeting may very well finish early. "I appreciate realistic agendas," says Jaffer. "If the meeting finishes early because we tackled all the topics, nobody complains." Hopefully, at the top of your meeting, individuals can feel better regarding the subject or project and have a lot of insight into following steps.

Some effective meeting strategies to help ensure that individuals leave your meeting with clarity and purpose include:

Sum up the meeting with notes and action items. Make these notes accessible to everybody who attended the meeting. Think about sharing notes with others who couldn't attend. Or record meetings when possible and

I Could Have Gotten That Via Email

acceptable and channelize a link to the audio or video after. This can be significantly valuable for team members operating remotely or companies with a globally distributed workforce.

Assign action items or things to follow up on to specific people whenever possible. It's additionally useful to schedule a point or a time with someone to check in on progress.

If there was a specific discussion that was tabled, make certain they're surfaced afterward therefore individuals will choose how, when, and if to keep them rolling.

Don't forget to channelize the occasional anonymous feedback form to measure how effective the meeting was for attendees. Survey your attendees! Ask them if the meeting was productive for them. How would they improve it? Was it a valuable use of their time? Use the Plus and Delta method works wonders! From the [Lean Construction Institute:](#) Plus/Delta is a quick, simple retrospective to improve meetings, planning sessions, or repetitive activities. By using Plus/Delta, teams can continuously improve meetings or activities and show respect for people by discussing the value of or ability to improve the time spent on events. I use the Plus and Delta method for all of my meetings!

Running effective meetings will feel like a large order, particularly once they're the default approach a company shares information. Too often, meetings ask for employees' time but not for his or her thoughts or skill set. By meeting only when required, crafting a solid agenda, priming individuals to pay attention deeply, being inclusive, and leaving with clear next steps, you'll be able to host effective meetings that leave everybody feeling impressed instead of pissed off.

I encourage you to get started today following these steps and plan your next outcome driven meeting!

@mjcsolutions

www.ingramcontent.com/pod-product-compliance
Lightning Source LLC
Chambersburg PA
CBHW041949240526
45473CB00036B/2798